L. A. Lehmann

I0018444

Location-based Mobile Games

State of the art and future challenges for developing location-based games for mobile devices

GRIN - Verlag für akademische Texte

Der GRIN Verlag mit Sitz in München hat sich seit der Gründung im Jahr 1998 auf die Veröffentlichung akademischer Texte spezialisiert.

Die Verlagswebseite www.grin.com ist für Studenten, Hochschullehrer und andere Akademiker die ideale Plattform, ihre Fachtexte, Studienarbeiten, Abschlussarbeiten oder Dissertationen einem breiten Publikum zu präsentieren.

Document Nr. V187510

L. A. Lehmann

Location-based Mobile Games

State of the art and future challenges for developing location-based games for mobile devices

GRIN Verlag

Bibliografische Information der Deutschen Nationalbibliothek: Die Deutsche Bibliothek verzeichnet diese Publikation in der Deutschen Nationalbibliografie; detaillierte bibliografische Daten sind im Internet über http://dnb.d-nb.de/ abrufbar.

1. Auflage 2012
Copyright © 2012 GRIN Verlag GmbH
http://www.grin.com
Druck und Bindung: Books on Demand GmbH, Norderstedt Germany
ISBN 978-3-656-11345-4

TECHNISCHE UNIVERSITÄT BERLIN

SEMINAR PAPER

Location-based Mobile Games

Author:
LA LEHMANN

January 23, 2012

Abstract

In the recent years location-based services have become more and more popular due to advanced mobile devices that make the use of these services very convenient. With the rise of location-based services location-based games will also gain popularity and become more wide spread.

This seminar paper describes game patterns and new game types that are possible with location based games. It also examines different techniques to determine the geolocation of players, and it analyses the changes to the game experiences known from traditional video games.

Ultimately this paper gives an overview of the current state of the art concerning location-based games and discusses several issues and possibilities concerning the implementation of one.

Contents

1 Introduction

The smart phone market has seen rapid development in the recent years. Since the first blackberry was introduced for business users in 1999, it took 8 years until smart phones were sold for the mass consumer market, beginning with the iPhone in 2007, as described by Hall et al. [1]. After the success of the iPhone many other vendors started offering smart phones for the mass market and, since CQ4 2010, more smart phones/tablets then computers/laptops have been sold [2].

Considering the size and growth of this market, it is only natural for the video game industry to offer games for smart phones. According to the iTunes charts for the best selling paid apps 2009 [3], the most sold games that year were ported versions of popular video games like e.g. the SIMS 3. From then on, the game industry started heavily utilizing smart phone specific features like the touch screen or the gyroscope. In particular, the touch screen is no longer only used to push buttons but it is used to create a different gaming experience, as for example done by the game "Fruit Ninja".
The iTunes charts for the following year [4] show that applications making heavy use of these features sell better. This trend continues in 2011 [5] indicating that consumers react positively to the utilization of these features.

With more powerful smart phones that are constantly connected to the Internet, it becomes possible to use other smart phone specific features for gaming. One of these features is the GPS sensor built into most currently available smart phones. Built-in functions to determine the phones position make it possible to change the game experience based on the geographical position of the player.
These location-based games can create an entirely new gaming experience. The game is no longer taking place in the living room, as it moves with the user. Different to traditional handheld video gaming devices, location-based games can incorporate the environment into the game thus blurring the line between game and reality. Heavy use of these features leads to a new way to play and also to new game design methods.
Besides the possibilities and chances that come with location-based gaming, this new kind of games also brings new challenges. Some of them are common for all applications on smart phones, like the sparse availability of resources, while others are specific for location-based games, like e.g. the verification of the player position.

The remainder of the paper is structured as follows. In Section 2 an overview is given over location-based services and location-based games. Section 2.1 shows different game patterns for location-based games and Section 2.6 names several purposes of location-based games where these patterns can be used. Several positioning systems and their

usage in location-based games are discussed in Section 3. Section 4 illustrates differences in the game experience between video games and location-based games. Finally, a conclusion is drawn in Section 5 and future challenges are pointed out in Section 6.

2 Overview

"Location-based Services (LBSs) are IT services for providing information that has been created, compiled, selected, or filtered taking into consideration the current locations of the users or those of other persons or mobile devices" [6]. Many applications for modern smart phones incorporate LBSs to provide location-based information. This information can be used to give location-based recommendations, provide navigation information, track movement, conveniently communicate the current location to friends, etc. However, it can also be used in the area of entertainment to create a new kind of games that makes the position of the player an essential part of the game.

A location-based game (LBG) is here defined as **a form of play that is designed to be played on a device in motion and changes the game experience based on the location**. To create a location-based experience usually a connection to other devices, e.g. a server or other players, is used. However, it is also possible for single player games to store all required information on the device itself. Thus a connection is not necessary for a device to run a location-based game as long as the game changes based on the device position.

In the following two sections game patterns and usage possibilities of LBGs are described. Table 2.1 gives an overview on how patterns are used in certain types of games.

2.1 Game Patterns of LBGs

To use the location in the game several game patterns or a combination of them can be used. In this chapter four common game patterns are analyzed. An graphical overview over these patterns is given in figure 2.1.

2.2 Search-and-Find

A popular pattern is the one here referred to as *Search-and-Find*. In this type of game the player has to find a certain geolocation. Finding the geolocation can involve the actual act of searching if only the rough location is given. However, the player can also be guided to the place by the game using some kind of navigation system within the game.

Instead of requiring the player to move to certain coordinates, it is also possible to let the player find a certain object, e.g. a school, a hospital, or a beer garden. In this case the player has a range of geolocations to choose from, depending on his surroundings

Game	Game Patterns				Usage Possibilities				
	Search-and-Find	Follow-the-Path	Chase-and-Catch	Change-of-Distance	Entertainment	Education	Physical Activity	Advertising	Data Acquisition
Geocaching [7]	X	-	-	-	X	-	X	-	-
Tourality [8]	-	X	-	-	X	-	X	-	-
FoxHunt [9]	-	-	X	-	X	-	-	-	-
Shadow Cities [10]	-	-	X	-	X	-	-	-	-
Mobile Hunters [11]	-	-	X	-	X	-	-	-	-
Botfighters [12]	-	-	X	-	X	-	-	-	-
The Journey [13]	-	-	-	X	X	-	-	-	-
Savannah [14]	-	-	-	X	X	X	-	-	-
CityExplorer [15]	X	-	-	-	X	-	-	-	X
FIASCO [16]	X	-	-	-	X	-	-	-	X

Table 2.1: Overview over several LBGs, their game patterns, and purpose

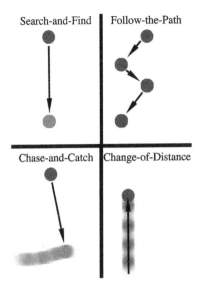

Search-and-Find	Follow-the-Path
Chase-and-Catch	Change-of-Distance

Figure 2.1: Graphical overview over the analyzed game patterns

and the size of the game field. This game pattern can for example be used in LBGs for data acquisition, as shown in section 2.11.

The basic concept behind the Search-and-Find game pattern is that the player has to reach a destination. This destination is always a fixed point in the game world, meaning that the geolocation for this specific destination does not change. This is also the case if no specific geolocation is given, since the player has then to choose from a range of locations which are fixed.

The most famous LBG genre using this pattern is geocaching [7]. In this type of games the player has to find an object which is hidden at certain GPS coordinates. This object is usually a real world box containing various items. The aim of the game is to find this box using the GPS coordinates, choose one of the items stored in the box, and in turn put a new item in the box.

2.3 Follow-the-Path

A game pattern very similar to Search-and-Find is the one here referred to as *Follow-the-Path*. Also in this game pattern the player has to reach a destination; however, the focus is not on the destination itself but on the way the player reaches it. It typically involves a certain route that the player has to follow, similar to a suggestion coming from

a navigation system. Different from a navigation system, the player commonly receives a penalty within the game if he does not follow the predefined route. The penalty depends on the advantage the player gets from leaving the route. This means that players that take shortcuts in location-based racing games usually lose the game immediately.

Besides a strict given route, it is also possible to not give any, but track the player's movement. Here the player can choose the route by himself but the movement still remains the core game objective. This is for example the case in a game where the player draws on a virtual game board by moving in the real world. In this game his destination is irrelevant since he or other players can just see the picture he painted by moving.

The route chosen by a player can also be recorded in order to find the best path between two points in a LBG for data acquisition.

The basic concept here is very similar to Search-and-Find with many consecutive points that the player has to reach or can set by himself.

One example here is the game Tourality [8] where the player has to complete a course in a certain time. Since this game pattern is often used for games focusing on physical activity further examples are given in section 2.9.

2.4 Chase-and-Catch

Chase-and-Catch, as defined by Misund et al. [9], is another popular pattern for LBGs. A Chase-and-Catch pattern requires the player to hunt a moving object in the game world. This object can be another player, making the game very similar to the traditional children's game tag, or a virtual thing only existing within the game world. Usually the player has to reach the object he is chasing or he has to get to know its current location in order to successfully catch it.

The basic concept here is that the destination is frequently changing. This can make the game more challenging for the user, depending on the frequency of changes and possible strategies to carry out the catch.

This pattern can be used in a single player environment with one player chasing one object, e.g. a hunter chasing a fox [9], or in a more complex multiplayer environment. This is for example done by the game Shadow Cities [10] where two groups of players have to "catch" each other with every player chasing and being chased at the same time.

2.5 Change-of-Distance

A less frequently used pattern is the one here referred to as *Change-of-Distance*. In contrast to the previously mentioned patterns, this pattern does not involve actually reaching a certain geolocation. The main goal is to get closer to a geolocation or further away. The location itself is not important; it is just the movement that matters. Another distinction is that the direction is not important either. While both Search-and-Find and Chase-and-Catch require the player to move in a certain direction to reach the objective, this is not the case in games using the Change-of-Distance pattern.

An example for a LBG using the Change-of-Distance pattern is The Journey, an adventure game where the player can read the next part of the story only after having moved a certain distance [13].

2.6 LBG Usage Possibilities

Traditional video games usually exist for the sole purpose of entertainment. Even though there are some games that also have an educational purpose, they usually still focus on entertainment and are far inferior to pure educational software. New video game systems that have been created to combine physical activity with gaming, like the Wii, still stay far behind real sport activities. While it is obvious that several video games or gaming systems have tried to promote other activities and give the player some benefits by playing, this goal has never been reached in an extent degree.

Of course all LBGs are still based on entertainment, since they are games and thus involve the act of playing. However, the location-based gameplay makes it possible to incorporate other aspects in a unique way.

Based on the already existing market and current research, the following areas have been chosen: entertainment, education, physical activity, advertising, and data acquisition.

2.7 Entertainment

As mentioned before, all games have the purpose to entertain. However, games in the commercial market usually solely focus on entertainment in order to generate the highest possible revenue.

There are very few examples of LBGs outside of research, since only recent smart phones fulfill the requirements to run games for the mass market.

One of the games that has been published in Q4 2011 is Shadow Cities [10]. In Shadow Cities the player takes the role of a magician fighting for one of the two factions in the game. He can then use magic spells to defeat hostile players or non-player characters. The factor of the location is included in the game in the way that the game world is an exact map of the real world and the player's character moves together with the player's smart phone.

Besides the games that are currently being published and use state of the art graphics, text based LBGs have been developed since Botfighters got published in 2000 [12]. In Botfighters, a Cell-ID based game, the player had to send a SMS to find nearby players. Once a player was found, he could be shot by sending another SMS.

2.8 Education

If LBGs are used for education, they have a unique possibility: connecting places and stories. Using the Search-and-Find game pattern it is possible to embed historical locations of a city or any other place into a game.

In this way the player can learn about history in a different way. One possible application could be a LBG taking place in East Germany after the Berlin Wall was built. In this scenario the player could take the role of an East German citizen, trying to escape to West Berlin. As part of the game, the player might have to go to Checkpoint Charlie to find out that he is not allowed to cross the border here but has to find a way to escape from East Germany. Within the game the player would learn about the process of getting an entry visa to West Berlin and abut flight attempts from East Berlin while visiting the historical places.

Another example is the LBG Savannah [14]. In this game children can learn how lions live and hunt in the African savannah. In the first part of the game the children play outside and move their character, a lion, on the virtual game field, the savannah, by moving themselves in the real world. After the hunt, they return to the classroom to discuss the events of the game.

The difference between a video game that tells the same story within a virtual world and a LBG is the closer link between game and reality in the latter. By visiting real places the story becomes more authentic and thus leads to a higher educational effect. This effect can be used to convey location specific knowledge in a more credible way. Since the knowledge has to be tied to a location in order to utilize this effect, the areas where LBGs can be used for education are limited. In areas like history education this is usually the case so that historical events can be told in a more lively way. However, it is very hard to connect locations with knowledge in more abstract areas like e.g. math or spelling. While it is also possible to convey knowledge which is not related to a location within a LBG, it is then not possible to utilize the beneficial effects of the connection between real world and game.

2.9 Physical Activity

Due to the steady increase in obesity and a lack of physical activity, gaming systems like the Wii or Kinect by Microsoft were developed to counter the problem. The idea was to combine physical activity with video games and promote exercising while playing a game. However, the required range of movement for these systems is very limited. Exercises usually take place in a small space in front of the gaming system and involve moving the body over a short distance. For this reason, they are not comparable to real world sports and fail in combating obesity.

LBGs on the other hand usually involve some form of movement. For this reason, physical activity is the core of these LBGs. Depending on the game the player has to move a great distance in order to proceed in the game.

One game that incorporates physical activity as core of the game is Tourality [8]. In this game players can create racing routes in the real world and make them available to other players. For every geolocation where a route is available a player can accept the challenge and start the race. The race is then completed by running along the path defined by the chosen route. Depending on the game mode the locations that create the route have to be reached in a different order. The common goal of all modes, however, is to complete the route as quickly as possible. Based on the time required to complete the route, a high score is created, challenging players to perform even better and complete the race faster.

This example shows that even though basic physical activity is part of every LBG, it can be the dedicated goal. In the case of Tourality it is the core of the game. However, due to the design of the application, it still is a game and thus it does not appear to the player in the same way as dedicated physical activity.

This shows that LBGs bear great potential in the sector of games for physical activity.

2.10 Advertising

Location data is already heavily used in location-based services to customize advertising for the current geolocation of the user. This shows the value of location-based services in advertising.

One option to use LBGs for advertising is to incorporate advertising in the game. This can be done by showing banner advertising depending on the location of the player. With this method it is possible to advertise local businesses and display offers in shops close to the player's geolocation.

Another option is to use a LBG to influence the real world movement of customers. For example a game could take place in a supermarket or mall. Within the game the player could collect some sort of tokens that are hidden at different places of the supermarket or mall. Upon completing the game the player could be awarded with a coupon or discount to use for this shop or all shops within the mall.

By offering the game for free and a giving a benefit for completing the mission, a lot of customers would play that game while shopping in order to receive the coupon or discount. The game operator can then place the tokens to direct the players to shelves with new products or products that are not sold as frequently as expected.

Since this game would take place indoors the positioning system has to be chosen adequately from table 3.1.

The range of possibilities and the potential increase in revenue by using LBGs for advertising indicate that LBGs will be used in the future to promote new products or

influence the movement of customers. The current high interest in the geolocation of smart phones users shows that the market volume for LBGs is very high.

2.11 Data Acquisition

A very unique possibility for LBGs is that they can be used for real world data acquisition. With the help of the users, data can be collected about the real world to create more accurate or more detailed maps. Using information from customers it is possible to give a geolocation a context. For example a building could be marked as a church or as tourist attraction. This data can then be integrated in a map to allow better navigation.
While collecting data is possible with all kind of location-based services, LBGs are ideally suited for this task. With this form of game it is possible to take an otherwise boring task and motivate users to carry it out by creating a game around it.

One example of a LBG for data acquisition is CityExplorer, as proposed by Matyas [15]. This game aims to collect data about the communication network and the geographic location. The data about the communication network consists mainly of available GSM-cells and their IDs. It also includes data about Wi-Fi access points. This data is then linked with data about the geographic location i.e. the GPS coordinates. Since this type of data can be collected by all kinds of location-based services, CityExplorer also aims to collect non-geographic data. Non-geographic data contains all information that is related to a real world object. One example is the purpose of the location, e.g. the information that a building at a certain geolocation is a hospital.
To gather the non-geographic data, an exploration approach is used. At the beginning the game board that correlates to the real world is empty and has to be uncovered step by step. To uncover a piece of the game board, a tile, players have to find a certain object within this tile. The objects that can be used are negotiated among the players before the game starts. They consist of important real world locations like beer gardens, hospitals, churches, etc. The players get points by reaching these positions. When a player reports being at one of these objects, the GPS coordinates are stored and a map is created based on the reports.

A similar game is FIASCO in which players compose a short scene out of pictures similar to improvisational theatre [16]. The goal of FIASCO is to build a new kind of map by publishing the scenes made by players. Using this alternative map one can see the places from a different perspective. To a certain degree this perspective represents how the person who created the scene sees this location. Thus it is possible to learn something about a place just by looking at this map.

13

3 Determining Player Positions

To determine the location of a mobile device several approaches exist. The currently, most frequently used methods are: GPS, Wi-Fi, cell tower triangulation, single cell tower, and IP, as listed by Wroblewski [17]. While other methods exist, such as the use of real world artifacts (section 3.5) or self-reported positioning (section 3.6), they are not (yet) heavily used in commercial applications.

(A-)GPS and the use of the cell tower network to gather data on the user location within games have been examined by Rashid et al. [12]. They compared different location-based games that have been released until 2005 showing that these games either use (A-)GPS or Cell ID to determine the player position.

An overview over methods that have been proposed by research or are already used in LBGs can be found in table 3.1.

3.1 (A-)GPS

Nowadays determining the location using a GPS sensor is still one of the most popular approaches due to its high accuracy. Because the GPS system only depends on the GPS satellites that send their signal from space, it is available everywhere, even in areas with no phone coverage or Internet. However, the accuracy is not very high when buildings obstruct the signal sent by the satellites. Especially inside buildings it can be very hard to determine the position, and the result might be inaccurate. Additionally, the required time to find the satellites is high. To decrease the required time to adjust to the satellites, assisted GPS (A-GPS) can be used. By downloading additional information about the location of the satellites from the Internet, it is possible to decrease the time required to adjust to the satellites. The problem with using GPS is that it consumes a lot of energy thus significantly decreasing the battery life of the smart phone.

3.2 Cell-ID

An alternative to GPS is geolocating the smart phone using Cell-ID. This system identifies the cell of the network provider that the smart phone is currently in. Since every cell of the mobile network has a unique ID, this ID is transmitted to the location service. The Cell-ID can then be mapped to a location. This method is not very accurate since the cells can be quite big, especially in rural areas, as shown in figure 3.1. However, cells

in large cities are smaller in order to handle the higher load caused by the higher population density. As network operators further decrease the cell size to handle more users with mobile Internet connections, the accuracy of the Cell-ID system might increase, especially in large cities.

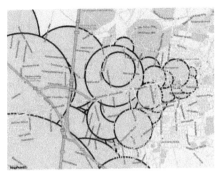

Figure 3.1: T-Mobile network cells in Darmstadt [11]

The accuracy of the Cell-ID is also very good within buildings. As long as the smart phone can get a signal from the network operator, it can determine the cell it is currently in. For this reason, the Cell-ID is sometimes used within buildings if it is not possible to receive an accurate GPS signal.

A more precise method using the cell phone network infrastructure is cell tower triangulation. If a phone receives the signal of at least three cell phone towers, it is possible to calculate the current location based on the estimated distance from each tower. This method is more accurate than only using the ID of one cell, but still less accurate then using GPS.

3.3 Wi-Fi Access Points

Similar to the Cell-ID, a Wi-Fi connection can be used. Since Wi-Fi only covers a small area, especially when used indoors, each Wi-Fi access point creates its own small cell. Similar to a Cell-ID, the MAC address of the access point can be used [18]. By using a database with known locations of Wi-Fi networks, the position of the user can be determined based on the Wi-Fi network whose signals can be received by the phone. The accuracy can be increased by approximating the distance to the access points. Furthermore multiple access points can be utilized using an algorithm similar to cell tower triangulation.

To create the database with the mapping of Wi-Fi access points to geolocations, wardriving is usually used. Companies like Skyhook [19] or Google [20] use special cars that drive through cities and collect data about Wi-Fi access points and their

position. For places like airports, where wardriving is not possible, the data can be collected manually. This mapping can also be made available by the operator of the Wi-Fi network.

Given that the location of the access point has been mapped, the accuracy depends on the size of the Wi-Fi "cell". If the location has not been mapped, it might be possible to determine the location of the Wi-Fi access point based on its IP. However, this is only possible if the smart phone is connected to the Wi-Fi network and has Internet access. Thus Wi-Fi positioning depends heavily on accurate mapping of all Wi-Fi access points in the area. Another problem is that Wi-Fi is very noise sensitive so that the approximation of distance can vary greatly.

3.4 IP Geolocating

A study by Balakrishnan et al. examined the usage of the IP address to geolocate a smart phone [21]. The result of the study is that it is impossible to determine the location solely based on the IP since it can change within one minute. Furthermore an experiment showed that the range of IP addresses for two devices is almost identical even if they are at entirely different locations. While the smart phone cannot be geolocated, it is possible to measure the round-trip time (RTT) in order to determine the distance between phone and server. Due to the low variance in RTT, this delay can be used in a location-based game where the player moves towards or away from a server.

Another result of the experiment was that the IP address always correlated to a gateway within the country where the smart phone was used. For this reason, the IP based approach might be used if only the country of origin has to be determined.

3.5 Real World Artifacts

Besides the previously discussed techniques, Rashid et al. propose the usage of RFID for location-based games [22]. As a proof of concept they designed the game PACLAN. The game is a version of Pac-Man where one player (Pac-Man) is hunted by several other players (ghosts). Before the game is started, RFID tags are placed in the game area and on the player's clothes. As soon as a player comes close to a RFID tag the mobile device he is carrying transmits the tag to the server which sends the player information about his position.

Another comparable approach using a Bluetooth server has also been implemented by Rashid et al. [23]. Instead of using RFID tags, a Bluetooth server is used to send messages to clients. Using this approach it is possible to create Bluetooth cells that are connected via a server to enable interaction with users in different areas. It is also possible to create peer-to-peer connections between users to decrease the load on the network.

This approach is very similar to using Cell-ID or Wi-Fi. The main difference here is that the "cells" are created when the game is set up. For this reason, the accurate

position of each cell is known to the server. The size of the cell is also known to the server, thus leading to more accurate positioning.

Instead of using RFID or Bluetooth, it is also possible to use other real-world items like QR-Codes. This requires the user to take pictures of the code and send it to a server. The server then queries a database with the exact geolocation of each QR-Code to determine the position of the user. For this reason, a QR-Code has to be placed at each location where the user has to determine his location. A big disadvantage of this method is that the user has to actively scan the code while with most other approaches it is possible to determine the location automatically.

One advantage of using real world items, like RFID tags, is the high power efficiency compared to using GPS. This is not necessarily true if QR-Codes are used, since the user has to take pictures of them which might be less energy efficient then using GPS, depending on the frequency in which QR-Codes have to be scanned. The advantage of both approaches is that the position is determined with a very high accuracy if enough tags are deployed on the game field. However, the game area has to be prepared thus increasing the cost for setting up and maintaining the game. Despite the advantages, these approaches should only be used if the game area is small or temporary.

3.6 Self-reported Positioning

Benford et al. [24] tested an entirely different approach in the game 'Uncle Roy All Around You'. Instead of relying on technical services to determine the position, users report their own position. Players were equipped with an interactive electronic map of the area and used this map to regularly report their position. This was done by tapping on the point of the map where the user thought to be located. While the downside of this approach is that players have to actively report their position, it performed sufficiently well for this game with a median distance error of 25 meters. The system is also very intuitive to use since it is very similar to navigating with a normal map. It also requires no additional power because no positioning systems are used.

3.7 Combination of Methods

Comparing all the mentioned methods to determine the geolocation of a smart phone, it can be said that the best way is a combination of different methods. In places with many buildings it is very hard to get a GPS signal and it can be inaccurate. Upon entering one of these buildings the accuracy will further decrease. However, areas with many buildings usually have a very high population density. For this reason, there are usually a number of households with Wi-Fi networks and several public Wi-Fi access points. In addition, the network cells will be small in order to handle the high amount of cell phone users.

In this environment the best solution is to use GPS outside of the building and Wi-Fi inside. If no Wi-Fi is available the Cell-ID could be used.

Skyhook for example combines Wi-Fi, GPS, and Cell-ID [19] to get the best results. This combination of positioning systems could be extended by using a Bluetooth server in certain locations where high accuracy is required, like in areas where a game objective has to be reached. Additionally, self reported positioning could be used in other areas, for example to help players organize themselves while not draining too much of their battery.

Method	Advantages	Disadvantages	Suggested Use
(A-)GPS	very high availability outdoors, very accurate outdoors (with A-GPS)	low availability indoors, low accuracy indoors, very high power consumption	All types of games, especially when played mainly outdoors
Cell-ID	high availability, low power cost	low accuracy	Games that can deal with inaccuracy like a Search-and-Find game for tourist attractions
Cell Tower Triangulation	high availability, low power cost	low accuracy (but higher then Cell-ID)	Games that can deal with inaccuracy like a Search-and-Find game for tourist attractions
Wi-Fi	low/no additional power cost (depending on the Wi-Fi positioning method)	low accuracy, low availability outside of cities	Games that take place in an environment with a lot of Wi-Fi networks for example at an airport
IP address	no additional power cost	only usable to approximate distance between user and server	Games that rely on distance, e.g. a game for travelers that changes as the player gets closer to his destination
RFID	high accuracy, same accuracy indoors, low power consumption	very expensive to set up, requires devices with RFID reader	Games on a small game field, e.g. educational games in a historic city district, temporary games for example to promote a product
Bluetooth server	high accuracy, same accuracy indoors, low power consumption, available on most phones (not limited to smart phones)	very expensive to set up	Games on a small game field, e.g. educational games in a historic city district, temporary games for example to promote a product
QR-Code	perfect accuracy, same accuracy indoors	expensive to set up (but cheaper then RFID/Bluetooth), inconvenient for users	Games on a small game field, e.g. educational games in a historic city district, temporary games for example to promote a product
Self-reported position	no additional energy cost	comparable low accuracy, inconvenient for users	Games that do not rely on accurate positioning and where correct reporting is in the interest of the user, e.g. sightseeing games

Table 3.1: Comparison of Methods to Determine the Player Position

4 Changes to the Game Experience

All traditional video games are played in front of the game console. Even if the game console is portable the player position is usually stationary. Since the player's position is changing in LBGs, the resulting game experience is different.

The major difference is in the areas of social interaction and connection between game and real world. This difference is due to the fact that the player's position is not stationary anymore but as moves a lot in a public space. While previously players only encountered other players' avatars, they now encounter other players in the real world, leading to a different level of social interaction. This social interaction also contributes to the closer link between game and real world. Since the player moves in reality, game elements become more real and the world might be perceived in a different way. The player is no longer just playing; he now is in the game or even part of the game. Depending on the amount in which real world artifacts, like the boxes in geocaching, are incorporated into the game the lines between game and reality are blurred to a certain extent.

4.1 Social Interaction

In a multiplayer video game the social interaction is always delimited by the game, at least to a certain extent. One of the basic means of communication is natural speech. Since most games only offer a text-based chat function, natural speech is not always available there. Even in games that offer a voice communication it is not assured that other players can hear the communication because it can always be switched off during the game, or the sound system of the gaming device can simply be turned off. This inability to communicate in a natural way distorts the game experience and makes it surreal. This perception is strengthened by the fact that the real world identity of a player is only known by his friends, while other players just encounter his avatar. The game world is thus perceived more as an anonymous world without rules then as a social platform like a meeting or a traditional form of non virtual play.

One effect of this surrealism and anonymity within multiplayer video games is the frequent disrespectful behavior between players. This aggressive insulting of other players has been coined "flaming" by the gaming community. The existence of a term for this behavior already indicates its frequent occurrence.

In a LBG the situation is very different since the players usually meet in person as soon as they are close enough. For this reason, they can communicate naturally and the player character loses its anonymity. Thus the game is more seen as a social event and players are more likely to adopt social norms within the game and when communicating

with each other.

In addition to the different type of communication between players, there are also other changes to the traditional game experience concerning the social interaction. As mentioned earlier, players of a LBG have the chance to meet in person and not just meet other players'. By playing the game they already have one common interest and thus it is easy for them to socialize and even become friends.

While friendships can also be developed within multiplayer video games, they usually stay within the game. Players who encounter each other in a multiplayer video game do not necessarily live close to each other. Usually the contrary is the case. For this reason, it is very hard to establish and maintain real world friendships.

Since players in a LBG already encounter in the real world, it is much easier to establish friendships or other social connections outside the game.

To show the tighter social bonding of players within an LBG, an experiment was conducted by Coe et al. [25]. They designed a location-based murder mystery game with the objective of allowing players to expand their social network. Within the game several groups were created. These groups then had the task to search for clues which could be exchanged in the game for virtual weapons and ammunition. The weapons and ammunition were used to "kill" another team which was declared as target by the game. Each team that got defeated had to move to a bar where they received one free alcoholic beverage, could chat, and got to know each other.

Results show that the teams communicated strongly with each other, even during combat. A survey conducted as part of the study indicated that most players enjoyed the game and networking with other players. It is remarkable that a follow-up survey, conducted one month later, showed that some players were still in contact with people they met during the game.

4.2 Perception of Real World

If a multiplayer video game is played, there is usually no interaction with the real world. All actions are solely carried out within the specific virtual game world. For this reason, the player might be able to change the virtual world, but his actions have no effect on the real world. While it might happen that the player associates locations in the game world with real events or emotions, this is not the case for any locations of the real world due to the strict separation of both worlds.

In a LBG the player moves and acts within the real world. For this reason there is no strict separation between game world and reality which can cause the player to percept his surroundings in a different way.

The thin border between game and reality is especially evident for location-based mixed reality games. In this type of game the play field is usually the entire world and the player can interact with the area where his current geolocation is. An example for

a game like this is Shadow Cities [10]. Besides fighting other players, it is also possible to cast spells within the game to change the game world. For example, the spell "ward" can be used to create a virtual defense tower that attacks enemies even if the player is not currently playing the game.

If a player sees this type of building constantly at the same position in the game world, he will perceive the corresponding location in the real word differently. His emotions and connection then depend on the effect of the building on his game character. For example, a building that offers protection in the game and is always on the same public square will cause the player to think of the square as a safe place. As a result, visiting this specific public square will cause positive emotions to the player, even if he is not currently playing the game. However, it can also effect the emotions of the player in a negative way. For example a player will avoid a place that cause him to lose energy or has other negative effects on his character in the game. If the player is used to avoid this geolocation he will also subconsciously avoid it if the game is switched off and he is not playing.

The result of this changing perception of the real world is that the game seems more real. Actions that the player takes in the real world can cause effects in the virtual world of the LBG. A basic example for this is the movement of the player in the real world, which causes his character to move in the virtual world. Vice versa, events in the virtual world have effects in the real world. For example a player that creates a virtual building to restore the energy of other players at a certain geolocation will change how this place is perceived by players that regularly use the beneficial effects. While the events from the virtual world do not directly affect the real world, they change the perception of it. Because of the strong link between game and reality the game experience in a well designed LBG is more intense than in a video game.

5 Conclusion

Location-based gaming offers great possibilities and makes it possible to implement innovative ways of playing, much different from traditional video games. This is especially the case for the areas of education and physical activity. Since LBGs are much more suited to convey educational knowledge and to encourage physical activity, it is to be expected that LBGs will be developed in the near future to satisfy the existing needs that game consoles like the Wii or educational video games have not satisfied yet.

Besides these two niche markets, LBGs will also gain a major share in the entertainment market. Due to the fuzzy border between game and real world, and because of the resulting changes to the game experience, players will get a closer connection to the LBG. For this reason, well designed LBGs will create stronger emotions and satisfy the player more than video games, thus increasing the demand for LBGs.

Future LBGs will profit from the advanced technology used in modern smart phones to integrate the player's position conveniently into the game. Moreover, the wide range of possible positioning systems, which has been successfully tested in research, shows that for every type of game a suitable positioning system can be found.

Because of the mentioned reasons, a wide range of different LBGs will be developed and published in the coming years. Due to their fundamental difference from traditional video games, they will change the way how gaming is seen and will show that playing digital games does not necessarily mean being trapped in a small room in front of a console. This development will open new markets and introduce new audiences to gaming.

6 Future Challenges

Since LBGs are very different from traditional games played on PC or video game consoles, they provide several challenges that have not yet been fully solved.

Naliuka et al. name battery, storage, user interface, and processing power constraints together with the problem of telling a story in a location-based environment as major challenges in LBGs [26]. While all kinds of smart phone games struggle with the constraints on storage, user interface, and processing power, the energy consumption of LBGs is commonly much higher.

In addition to these challenges, Lonthoff et al. mention the problem of delimiting the game field [11] and Benford et al. mention uncertainty of accuracy [14] as another challenge for LBGs.

Furthermore, the problem of location cheating is discussed here. He et al. [27] already showed that location cheating is possible in location-based social networks. Since cheating is one of the major problems for competitive video games it is to be expected that competitive LBGs will face the same problem.

6.1 Energy Consumption

Energy consumption is one of the major unsolved challenges of LBGs. Commonly LBGs rely on GPS to a certain degree in order to accurately geolocate the player. However, this increases considerably the energy consumption. If the battery is drained too quickly by playing the game, the user might refrain from playing the game in the future. Additionally, some types of games, that involve long sessions of play, will not be playable if the phone runs out of battery during the game.

The problem of high power consumption is most dominant when (A-)GPS is used as a positioning system. To decrease the power consumption of GPS systems, several methods have been proposed (e.g. [28], [29]). The solution proposed by Paek et al. involves querying the location less frequently to reduce the power consumption. The core of most solutions is to use an algorithm or a different positioning system to reduce the queries made by the GPS system. Consequently this decreases the accuracy of the GPS system.

A temporary solution is to choose another positioning system which requires less energy and might still be suitable for the game, as shown in table 3.1. While the energy consumption of some positioning systems is lower than GPS, the overall energy consumption still exceeds the one of the normal phone usage.

However, increased energy consumption might not be a major problem in the future since the overall battery life is increasing with new generations of smart phones. Since better batteries are used with new smart phones while the energy consumption of the GPS receiver does not increase, the influence on battery life time might not be that dramatic in the future.

6.2 (In)Accuracy of Positioning Systems

Another challenge for LBGs is the accuracy (or inaccuracy) of positioning. This is especially the case in a multiplayer game using the Chase-and-Catch game pattern. If the players have to catch each other and the positioning system is not accurate, the task might be very hard to accomplish. Especially in a game where the player has to follow a certain path a system with high inaccuracy will make it impossible to play the game.

Usually this problem is closely linked to the problem of energy consumption. Positioning systems that are more accurate usually consume more energy or require more time to set up the game field.

But even a highly accurate positioning system usually involves several meters of inaccuracy which have to been handled by the game.

6.3 Location-based Cheating

A problem with LBGs is that the position is ultimately reported by the user's device. A malicious user could alter the game to manually send GPS coordinates, Cell-ID, or Wi-Fi access points to the game server. Since there is no possibility to constantly verify the position of all players in most positioning systems, cheating cannot be tracked. If the player moves at reasonable speed, the game system has no chance to discover that the position is not correct.

It has been shown by He et al. [27] that, besides manipulating the device, an emulator could be used to send false information. In this case the emulator was used to successfully circumvent the anti-cheating mechanism of the social network Foursquare and send false information.

Especially in multiplayer Chase-and-Catch games, it can lead to frustration and confusion if the game shows that two players are very close to each other, but the player who is sending false locations cannot be seen. Location-based cheating is also critical in LBGs whose purpose is advertising. If many users modify their position, the game cannot fulfill its purpose anymore.

The problem of location-based cheating is very similar to the problem of inaccuracy of the positioning system. The only difference here is that the inaccuracy is maliciously caused by the user. The main problem, however, is that games have to handle the inaccuracy without punishing honest users but, at the same time, punish users that cause inaccuracy or use it to their advantage.

A related problem is the use of unintended means of transport by the player. For example a player could use a bike to complete a race in the game Tourality [8] at a

much higher speed. While video games limit the movement speed of the player's avatar programmatically this is not the case for a LBG. On the one hand setting limits for the movement speed will frustrate players that move very fast, while on the other hand no limits might encourage players to move by car instead of walking.

6.4 Telling a Story

The challenge to tell a story based on the geolocation of the users is also mentioned by Rashid et al. [12]. This problem is commonly solved by embedding the geolocations of the story into the system. This can either be done within the software or by using real world artifacts like e.g. QR-Codes or RFID chips. Setting the positions can also be crowd sourced, thus allowing players to add new locations or routes, as for example done by Tourality [8].

Gustafsson et al. however suggest evolving the story based on the journey of the player, not simply on his geolocation [30]. This solution is only possible if traveling is a major part of the game.

6.5 Delimiting the Game Field

The problem with the game field is that some limits have to be provided by the game. In a video game the game world is created by the game designers and it is not possible to leave the game world. This is not the case with a LBG, especially if GPS coordinates are used that are valid worldwide. Thus the game field of a LBG is the entire world if no delimiters are put in place. This can lead to the problem that the player can start the game but no content or opponent is available at his location. Especially commercial games, which do not define a game field by purpose in order to be played all around the world, face this problem.

This problem can be solved by defining a game field and measuring if the player is within the field or at least reasonably close to it. A method to decrease the time needed to set up the game field is using color maps to quickly define the game field [31]. In this case it was possible to set up the game field in different cities within hours by giving playable areas a certain color.

Bibliography

[1] S. Hall and E. Anderson, "Operating systems for mobile computing," *Journal of Computing Sciences in Colleges*, vol. 25, no. 2, pp. 64–71, 2009.

[2] M. Murphy and M. Meeker, "Top mobile internet trends," in *Kleiner Perkins Presentation, February 10, 2011 at Google Think Mobile Conference¡ http://www. slideshare. net/kleinerperkins/kpcb-top-10-mobile-trends-feb-2011¿ (accessed April*, vol. 14, 2011.

[3] Gamasutra, "Apple reveals top-selling, high-rated iphone games of 2009," 2009, [Online; accessed 5-November-2011]. [Online]. Available: http://www.gamasutra.com/view/news/26431/Apple_Reveals_TopSelling_HighRated_iPhone_Games_of_2009.php

[4] Gigaom, "itunes rewind 2010 highlights top apps, app trends," 2010, [Online; accessed 5-November-2011]. [Online]. Available: http://gigaom.com/apple/itunes-rewind-2010-highlights-top-apps-app-trends/

[5] Apple, "itunes charts," 2011, [Online; accessed 5-November-2011]. [Online]. Available: http://www.apple.com/itunes/charts/paid-apps/

[6] A. Kupper, *Location-based Services: Fundamentals and Operation*. John Wiley & Sons, 2005.

[7] G. T. O. G. G. C. H. Site, "Videos: What is geocaching?" 2012, [Online; accessed 19-January-2012]. [Online]. Available: http://www.geocaching.com/videos/default. aspx#cat=cat:newbies&vid=-4VFeYZTTYs

[8] Tourality, "Tourality - the ultimate outdoor gps game," 2011, [Online; accessed 12-December-2011]. [Online]. Available: http://www.tourality.com/

[9] G. Misund, H. Holone, J. Karlsen, and H. Tolsby, "Chase and catch-simple as that?: old-fashioned fun of traditional playground games revitalized with location-aware mobile phones," in *Proceedings of the International Conference on Advances in Computer Enterntainment Technology*. ACM, 2009, pp. 73–80.

[10] G. Area, "Shadow cities - magical location based mmorpg for iphone, ipod touch and ipad," 2011, [Online; accessed 27-November-2011]. [Online]. Available: http://www.shadowcities.com/

[11] J. Lonthoff and E. Ortner, "Mobile location-based gaming as driver for location-based services (lbs)-exemplified by mobile hunters," *INFORMATICA-LJUBLJANA-*, vol. 31, no. 2, p. 183, 2007.

[12] O. Rashid, I. Mullins, P. Coulton, and R. Edwards, "Extending cyberspace: location based games using cellular phones," *Computers in Entertainment (CIE)*, vol. 4, no. 1, p. 4, 2006.

[13] Mopius, "The journey - a mobile location based adventure," 2011, [Online; accessed 14-December-2011]. [Online]. Available: http://journey.mopius.com/

[14] S. Benford, "Future location-based experiences," *JISC Technology and Standards Watch. Available at: http://www, jisc. ac. uk/techwatch*, 2005.

[15] S. Matyas, "Playful geospatial data acquisition by location-based gaming communities," *The International Journal of Virtual Reality*, vol. 6, no. 3, pp. 1–10, 2007.

[16] M. Chang and E. Goodman, "Fiasco: game interface for location-based play," in *Proceedings of the 5th conference on Designing interactive systems: processes, practices, methods, and techniques.* ACM, 2004, pp. 329–332.

[17] L. Wroblewski, "Mobile first," *LukeW Ideation+ Design*, 2010.

[18] Y. Chen, Y. Chan, and C. She, "Enabling location-based services in wireless lan hotspots," *International Journal of Network Management*, vol. 15, no. 3, pp. 163–175, 2005.

[19] I. Skyhook, "Skyhook: How it works - overview," 2011, [Online; accessed 25-November-2011]. [Online]. Available: http://www.skyhookwireless.com/howitworks/

[20] Google, "Location-based services," 2012, [Online; accessed 19-January-2012]. [Online]. Available: http://support.google.com/maps/bin/answer.py?hl=en&answer=1725632

[21] M. Balakrishnan, I. Mohomed, and V. Ramasubramanian, "Where's that phone?: geolocating ip addresses on 3g networks," in *Proceedings of the 9th ACM SIGCOMM conference on Internet measurement conference.* ACM, 2009, pp. 294–300.

[22] O. Rashid, P. Coulton, R. Edwards, and W. Bamford, "Utilising rfid for mixed reality mobile games," in *Consumer Electronics, 2006. ICCE'06. 2006 Digest of Technical Papers. International Conference on.* IEEE, 2006, pp. 459–460.

[23] O. Rashid, P. Coulton, and R. Edwards, "Providing location based information/advertising for existing mobile phone users," *Personal and Ubiquitous Computing*, vol. 12, no. 1, pp. 3–10, 2008.

[24] S. Benford, W. Seager, M. Flintham, R. Anastasi, D. Rowland, J. Humble, D. Stanton, J. Bowers, N. Tandavanitj, M. Adams *et al.*, "The error of our ways: the experience of self-reported position in a location-based game," *UbiComp 2004: Ubiquitous Computing*, pp. 70–87, 2004.

[25] J. Coe and M. Chen, "Making friends by killing them: using location-based urban gaming to expand personal networks," in *Proceedings of the 28th of the international conference extended abstracts on Human factors in computing systems*, ser. CHI EA '10. New York, NY, USA: ACM, 2010, pp. 3553–3558. [Online]. Available: http://doi.acm.org/10.1145/1753846.1754017

[26] K. Naliuka, T. Carrigy, N. Paterson, R. Cotton, S. K. Jensen, and M. Haahr, "Supporting immersive location-based games on resource-constrained platforms," in *Proceedings of the 7th International Conference on Advances in Computer Entertainment Technology*, ser. ACE '10. New York, NY, USA: ACM, 2010, pp. 102–103. [Online]. Available: http://doi.acm.org/10.1145/1971630.1971662

[27] W. He, X. Liu, and M. Ren, "Location cheating: A security challenge to location-based social network services," in *Distributed Computing Systems (ICDCS), 2011 31st International Conference on*, june 2011, pp. 740 –749.

[28] J. Paek, J. Kim, and R. Govindan, "Energy-efficient rate-adaptive gps-based positioning for smartphones," in *Proceedings of the 8th international conference on Mobile systems, applications, and services*. ACM, 2010, pp. 299–314.

[29] U. Bareth and A. Küpper, "Energy-efficient position tracking in proactive location-based services for smartphone environments," in *Proceedings of the IEEE 35th Annual Computer Software and Applications Conference (COMPSAC 2011)*. Munich, Germany: IEEE, Jul 2011, pp. 516–521. [Online]. Available: http://dx.doi.org/10.1109/COMPSAC.2011.72

[30] A. Gustafsson, J. Bichard, L. Brunnberg, O. Juhlin, and M. Combetto, "Believable environments: generating interactive storytelling in vast location-based pervasive games," in *Proceedings of the 2006 ACM SIGCHI international conference on Advances in computer entertainment technology*. ACM, 2006, p. 24.

[31] M. Flintham, "Painting the town red: configuring location-based games by colouring maps," in *Proceedings of the 2005 ACM SIGCHI International Conference on Advances in computer entertainment technology*. ACM, 2005, pp. 9–18.